# INUNDATED

# INUNDATED

Redeeming the Untruths of Dating and Purity
Culture in a Broken World

## LAUREN FAITH RYALS

RESOURCE *Publications* · Eugene, Oregon

INUNDATED
Redeeming the Untruths of Dating and Purity Culture in a Broken World

Resource Publications
An Imprint of Wipf and Stock Publishers
199 W. 8th Ave., Suite 3
Eugene, OR 97401

www.wipfandstock.com

PAPERBACK ISBN: 978-1-7252-7893-6
HARDCOVER ISBN: 978-1-7252-7894-3
EBOOK ISBN: 978-1-7252-7895-0

09/17/21

To my husband, Bryce
You are the most tangible representation
of the Gospel to me on this earth.

# Contents

# Introduction

The enemy was super tedious in the publishing process of this book. Between big life happenings, a computer with half of my work on it crashing a few weeks before my deadline, and a ton of doubt, I know that what is on these pages are a threat to Satan's desires. I had so much fear going into this and quite honestly, a lack of peace at most times. I feared that no one would desire to read it because of my age or lack of authority. I feared that it would be looked down upon, and I believed so many more lies throughout this process. But here we are, and here you are, reading it! I can't believe it has come to fruition; I wish I could sit across from you at a coffee shop and tell you about all of the things that went wrong during the process of writing and publishing this. I also wish I could sit across from you and hear your story and background on relationships, and learn why you have picked up this book.

My prayer as I was putting words onto paper was that any words that were not from the Lord would not make it on the pages, and that I would only be a vessel for furthering God's Kingdom. Satan hates Godly relationships, he hates couples that glorify the Lord through their love. And I pray that this book is a weapon that equips you to make Satan mad in your relationship endeavors and love life!

My generation has been so overwhelmed, and *inundated*, if you will, with all of the wrong examples and relationships to guide them in a love life that is pleasing to the Lord. We have been given the idolatry of sex, hookup and toxic purity culture, and the prevalence of divorce to be our guide, and that is just not the way God intended it.

In order to do relationships well, we need to look to Scripture and God's character to reveal *his* desires for our relationships. I pray that as you read through these pages, you are filled with a peace that surpasses all understanding, conviction where it's needed, and encouragement to rethink relationships how you always have. You are in for a wild one, a deep dive into my past, how I was raised in regard to relationships, and how my views have been flipped upside down through God's Word.

May you be inundated only with the truth.

# 1

# Flying Solo

Leonardo da Vinci was single. Sir Isaac Newton was single. Queen Elizabeth I was single. Beethoven, along with the Wright Brothers were both single. Paul, arguably the greatest evangelist and missionary of all time, was single.

*Jesus* was single.

I could go on and on, but you get the point. Our society, for centuries, has treated singleness like a disease, a chronic dark cloud over someone's life, an impediment or disability even. But what if I told you it was the exact opposite and that was far from the actual truth? What if I told you that singleness can be an asset in your life? I can practically feel the eyes rolling as you're reading this. In this chapter, as we begin this journey of dissecting what a Christlike love life truly looks like, the first lie I want to debunk is the lie that singleness is a negative thing.

In fact, in 1 Corinthians 7, when Paul is writing his letter to the people of Corinth, he says this:

> *I wish that all of you were as I am. But each of you has your own gift from God; one has this gift, another has that. Now to the unmarried and the widows I say: It is good for them to stay unmarried, as I do.* (1 Cor 7:7–8)

In this verse, we see Paul is actually telling the church that he wishes that everyone had the time he does to devote to ministry because of singleness. When Paul says that he wishes that they were like he is, he is referring to his relationship status. Singleness, just like marriage, is a gift in and of itself that is used to further God's kingdom, and one is no better than the other.

Nearly everything in our modern-day society is structured around and devoted towards couples and relationships. Almost every movie and television show involve romance in the plot line. We have magazines, podcasts, sermon series, product lines/brands—all devoted to the idea of being in a relationship with a significant other. Oftentimes, it can be an ultimatum or expectation for certain areas of professions and career paths. Rarely ever do we see an unmarried man leading a church as a pastor, or in a position of authoritative leadership in ministry.

So, where did we go wrong as a society? When did we mix singleness up with being a disease rather than the precious gift that it is? How can we shift what has been engrained in our minds for generations?

To answer these hard but necessary questions, we have to go to Scripture.

It is relatively easy to point the root of our distorted view of singleness back to the fall of man in Genesis. After all, this is where all of the world's issues ultimately stem from when you get to the root of them: sin. However, rather than leaving you with a vague answer there, let's dissect this some. In Genesis 2, when God created Eve for Adam, because "it is not good for the man to be alone," we see the beauty of relationships being born. We see how God did not see fit for the Earth to just have male, so he created female too. This is undoubtedly a beautiful thing. In fact, God followed his creation of man by saying it was "very good," unlike how he followed all other creation by saying it was just "good."

However, when this becomes distorted and twisted by sin, we start to turn the beautiful creation of relationships into idols in our lives. We increasingly grow fixated on the idea of having companionship with the opposite sex, and over time the idea that singleness is a negative thing seeps into our minds and hearts.

Through Paul's letters to the church, we see several positive sides to singleness that prove it to be just as valuable as a Godly relationship. One, we see that singleness is a gift to be received from

God just like marriage. Singleness doesn't define a person, just like marriage doesn't define a couple. Singleness simply is a relational state, and something we receive from God as a gift and product of His love and grace to us. Things start to change when our perspective shifts to singleness being a gift. Secondly, Paul speaks clearly of the advantages that singleness holds, such as the use of time and resources for complete and devout devotion to ministry and building God's kingdom. In 1 Corinthians 14:32–34, Paul shares that when a couple is in a marriage relationship, their desires and interests are divided. When you are single, you have the freedom and means to do things without having to worry about another individual the way you do when you are in a marital covenant with someone.

It is also important to realize that just like singleness can be hard, marriage can often be even harder. Many people believe this false reality that once they are married, their sin struggles will fade away, when in reality, they will be brought to light in marriage. Once a couple enters into marriage, their sinfulness is exposed more than ever before, and along with this comes many struggles.

Some people may indeed be called to singleness, but friend, it's not always permanent. In Psalms 37:4, we are told that when we delight in our relationship with the Lord, he will give us the desires of our hearts. This verse can be tainted and twisted quite often, but the important thing to remember is the more that we delight in and spend time with the Lord, the more our desires start to line up with what he desires for us.

To begin to shift this mindset that has been inscribed onto our society's standard for generations, we have to understand what singleness really is meant for. Once we realize the true beauty that singleness is, we can then begin to see the divine purpose that Jesus has for singles in this season. It's not until then that we can truly begin to recognize the gift that flying solo really can be in our lives.

If you are in a season of singleness right now, thank God for the gift of singleness, even if you feel like it's anything but a gift. The purpose of singleness is not to wait around for the perfect guy or girl to walk your way, but to spend this time truly seeking to become the best you can be for that guy or girl if and when they do come. Do all you can in this season to become more like Jesus.

Singleness can easily serve to be a breeding ground for selfishness and sin if not careful. But when you intentionally spend this time in your life not just waiting passively but actively seeking to become the person you want to be once the waiting is over, the harvest will be plentiful in your walk with Jesus. This is the only time in your life that you can truly just focus on becoming the best, most Christ-like version of yourself that you can possibly be. No distractions, no other person to get you sidetracked. While waiting periods can be brutal and hard, and growing impatient is the easiest thing to do, do not neglect to recognize that Jesus is in the waiting too. He isn't absent while you're waiting on something to come your way. It is crucial that you keep your eyes fixed on Heaven, because that is the ultimate relationship, the one that will sustain you forever.

I'd like to pose a question to you: what would your life look like in complete contentment? What would it look like if you genuinely took to heart the Scripture in 1 Peter 5 when we're told that we can cast all of our anxieties onto Jesus, because he cares for us?

What would your life look like without any fear at all?

I'm confident that this would be a gamechanger for every single person out there. When you begin to rest in the truth of God's faithfulness and his fulfilled promises, the presence of fear becomes less and less prevalent. I know what it's like to abide in fear and not peace, in anxiety and not calmness. It's enslaving, restricting, and it robs us of our true identity as children of our sovereign Lord.

One of the sweetest promises that Jesus has for us is that he never settles on his kids. Therefore, we cannot settle on ourselves. This not only refers to your search for a significant other, but also whether or not you choose to abide in fear or in peace. This is something that has been instilled in me ever since I was a young tween. When I was in sixth grade, my Sunday school teacher had each one of us girls make a list of attributes we wanted in our future husbands. After we were finished, she took them and prayed over them—she still does that to this day. Now, my list probably looked a little different compared to what it would've looked like had I made it today; but nonetheless, the notion is still the same.

Pray specifically. Pray fervently. Pray expectantly. Jesus never settles on His children.

To end this chapter, I asked some people, single, dating, engaged and married, what they wish they would've been told regarding singleness. Here is what they had to say:

> *"I wish when I was younger someone would have told me to embrace my season even if it felt heavy, because there is joy and grief in every season. I wish that I was told that I could be used by God in a great capacity; that just because I didn't have a relationship didn't mean that my 'usefulness' in the kingdom was dependent upon my dating or not dating."*

*"I wish I would have believed that I was enough, and that a man was not required, to complete me. SO grateful to now know that Jesus is all I need!"*

*"To guard your heart for the treasure it is (Proverbs 4:23)."*

*"I didn't marry until I was thirty. My siblings were married and having children and I felt so forgotten about. I wish someone had told me that it was just a season in my life for the Lord to prepare me to be a wife and mother someday. Also, not to rush into marriage. Marriage is wonderful and rewarding, but it is also work and you have to have stick-to-itiveness. Treasure your single years and then one day you will have marriage years to treasure all the more. Life is a marathon, not a sprint."*

*"I wish I would have been told that I am enough and waiting on God to send me that one man that he created just for me would be worth the wait. I wish I had spent that time I carelessly wasted on the wrong relationships and rooted myself in God's word and purpose he had for me then. Yet Thank God, HE was patient and waited on me and still brought to me the man he created for me. HE is amazing like that. Wish I had known that then."*

> *"Still working on absorbing this truth myself, but I wish I'd been told that there is time. There is time for a relationship and children and a career and all of those things. Don't rush it. You are a prize of high value and the Lord will bring someone along at the right time who will cherish you as he made you to be. He's already prepared your future, so enjoy who you are right now and until your season of*

*singleness ends, appreciate your individuality and learn who you are in Christ."*

If you're in a season of being single, I hope all or some of these words encourage you right where you're at. Remember, Jesus has you right where you're at for a reason, but he loves you way too much to leave you there.

## 2

# Incomplete

With the long list of relationship clichés, sweet nothings, and phrases often uttered in wedding vows comes phrases such as "you complete me," "you make me whole," and "you're my everything." These statements couldn't be more wrong, and in order to debunk them, it is vitally important to remember these passages of Scripture while reading through the next few pages.

*John 15:5:* "I am the vine; you are the branches. If you remain in me and I in you, you will bear much fruit; apart from me you can do nothing."

*1 Timothy 6:6–8:* "But godliness with contentment is great gain. For we brought nothing into the world, and we can take nothing out of it. But if we have food and clothing, we will be content with that."

*1 Thessalonians 5:23–24:* "May God himself, the God who makes everything holy and whole, make you holy and whole, put you together—spirit, soul, and body—and keep you fit for the coming of our Master, Jesus Christ. The One who called you is completely dependable. If he said it, he'll do it!"

Each of these excerpts from Scripture speak to the fact that our wholeness, contentment, and worth come from Jesus alone. Nothing on this earth can make you whole, complete you, or eternally satisfy you the way that Jesus can. We were all born with a God-sized hole in our hearts. What happens if you try to put a square peg in a round hole? It either doesn't fit, or there are parts left empty. This is what happens when we try and fill ourselves up with earthly relationships. When we try and put the temporary things of this earth into the God-sized hole made for only eternal things, we are left empty.

Growing up, it was instilled into me from an early age that before I decided to date, or pursue a romantic relationship, I needed to be completely whole and satisfied in Jesus. This wasn't taught to me just in regard to relationships either, but the importance of it in general as a Christ follower.

My dating "philosophy" has fallen in line with that ever since. If I am completely whole and content in the woman that God made me, with Jesus by my side independently, then if there is going to be another person in my life, they need to be an asset. If there is going to be someone that comes and walks alongside of me in a relationship, they cannot take away from the person God made me to be, because in the end, as harsh as it may sound, I don't need them in the first place.

Why waste time and energy on a broken sinner who is hindering rather than helping my walk with Jesus—the only one who makes me whole and satisfies my soul?

When we say phrases like I mentioned before, we nurture and foster a heart posture of codependency and not feeling adequate unless we have a significant other by our side.

I often get asked how you know if you're ready to date or not. One of the main answers I always give is that you should only start entertaining the idea of dating if you're happy and more than content alone in your singleness. It's not smart, and—frankly—dangerous for your soul if you begin to date someone when you aren't content being on your own. This not only hurts and negatively affects you in the end, but it also puts the other person at an extreme disadvantage, because they were never meant to fulfill you.

If you go into a dating relationship when you aren't satisfied in Jesus, you are trying to fill a void that can only be filled with Jesus. This results in hurt, heartache, confusion, and unfulfilled expectations that the other person never signed up for in the first place.

Now, to perform a little heart check on yourself, since you may be wondering or asking yourself if you hold this tainted heart posture, here are some questions you can ask yourself to begin assessing:

*"In seasons of singleness, are there moments where I am constantly looking or seeking out a relationship?"*

*"Do I ever feel impatient when someone brings up or questions my relationship status?"*

*"Do I feel overly envious of other people in my life who are in a relationship? Are there more moments of envy than being happy for them?"*

*"Have I gone more than a few months without dating just to focus on myself?"*

I could go on and on, but these few questions are good starting points to prompt your thinking on answering honestly. I would also recommend asking others in your life who know you well or are around you often if they notice you being overly focused on being in a relationship. Having this impatient heart posture can often blind us or distort our vision from being able to truly and clearly assess ourselves.

So, now that you may have an idea of where your heart is at, it begs the question of "what do I do in a prolonged season of waiting and desiring a relationship?"

First, I want to be quick to reassure you that it is not sinful, wrong, or even abnormal to desire a relationship. This is the way God wired each and every human, to desire community. What is wrong is when we begin to idolize the thought of being in a relationship or getting married. When this happens, we begin to lose ourselves in what can be a beautiful waiting period of refining, growing in confidence, and becoming closer to our Creator.

There is a song by Bethel Music that has the lyric "He's in the waiting." This has always been such a beautiful reminder to me in periods where I am beginning to grow impatient with God or others. It serves as a timely reminder that when our focus is tainted, we can miss God, especially in periods when he seems far, like he often does while we're waiting on something.

# INUNDATED

When you find yourself in a waiting period of any kind, but especially one where you're desiring a relationship, it is vital to be in constant communication with God, through prayer and diving into his Word. This is a prime time for you to focus even more intently on what he is trying to show and teach you. If you can't direct your attention on Jesus while you're single, it will prove to be even harder when you are in a relationship with another person.

# 3

# How Long Do I Have to Wait?

We live in a society of one to two-day Prime shipping, same day delivery, Postmates, Shipt, curbside pick-up, and fast food as the norm. All of these things have something in common: they happen fast and are a product of the ever-present "I want it now" mentality of today's culture. I would like to go out on a limb and say that this applies to our relationships as well. Resolve takes patience. Purity takes patience. Committing your soul to another human's soul takes patience. Things that don't take patience and are a result of the quick-fix culture we live in are casual sex, multiple marriages, and cohabiting before marriage. We want the wife and husband privileges before we have a wife or husband.

In singleness, this can also look like growing angry or bitter towards the fact that God hasn't opened the door for a relationship. We, as a society, despise waiting. If there is one fruit of the Spirit we are desperately lacking, in my opinion, it is that of patience. Because of this phenomenon, we tend to let this spirit of impatience trickle into our desires for and attitudes towards relationships. Hookup culture and "no strings attached" relationships are also byproducts of this. Anything that takes effort, work, and—most importantly—time, is something that is dreaded and scoffed at.

In relationships, impatience can lead to settling, arguments, and in some cases, divorce. This heart posture is detrimental to our own spiritual and relational health. Just like I mentioned in the last chapter, the fruit we produce is a direct result of the seeds we are planting with our thoughts and our actions. A heart posture of discontentment, bitterness, or impatience leads to an unsettled heart and a life of being let down when all God is asking you to do is be patient.

When I study fruits of the Spirit or seek to learn more about qualities that God desires for his children to have and embody, I like to specifically look at people in the Bible who embodied these things. I am a firm believer that we learn by doing and studying others' doing as well.

A few people in the Bible who embodied the virtue of patience in beautiful ways are Job, Joseph, and Abraham. These men are probably familiar names to you if you have grown up in church or studied the Bible at all.

When you look at Job, which actually is one of my favorite books in the Bible, you see a picture of longsuffering and endurance. You see a man who sought to honor God no matter the sacrifice, turmoil, or cost. I fell in love with the story of Job when I was in the midst of the darkest season I have ever experienced in my life thus far. I was just beginning on my journey of battling clinical mental illness and if you are familiar with Job in any way, you know he was well acquainted with hardship and mental anguish.

Job's story is one of fierce biblical patience. This is one of the few places in the Bible where there is a documented conversation between God and Satan.

To paraphrase, God found Satan roaming the earth, and asked if he had considered God's servant, Job. Job was described as a man of integrity who feared evil, insinuating that if Job was tested, he would not fall victim to turning from God based on the devil's tactics. God then told Satan that he could do what he wanted with Job, except take his life.

When you read on, you see that Job pretty much lost everything *but* his life. He suffered from medical issues that attacked his skin and afflicted his body. He lost his home, his children, his financial standing. He suffered more in a short span than most do in their entire lifetime. Yet, despite the trials and heartache, Job was patient with God. He knew that his peace and resolve was coming. He never cursed God, despite being asked to by his own wife.

He remained relentlessly faithful, stood strong, and never wavered. The fruit of patience that Job was delighting in was a direct reflection of his honor for God. And for it, he was blessed double fold what he lost in the end.

We can learn a lot from Job. Job did not know when or if his trial was ever going to be over, just like you may not know when this season of singleness will end. You have to remain steadfast and wait on the Lord.

Another person we can learn from is Joseph. Joseph was a man who, from an early age, felt a calling from God to be a leader to his people. He was described as being a man who was righteous and feared the Lord. Joseph knew God had him in a place preparing his heart and life for leadership. But Joseph was taken into slavery by his own brothers. Throughout his time in captivity, he was faithfully patient. He never turned from God; he nurtured the fruit of patience and was confident that God would fulfill his promise. Eventually, God did indeed lift Joseph up into great power and responsibility. And not only would God transform what the enemy meant for evil and turn it to good by allowing Joseph to lead over the Egyptians, but he would ultimately be in power over his own people, including the brothers that sold him into slavery.

This journey took patience, and God fulfilled every promise he made to Joseph and exceeded all expectations.

Lastly, I want to share with you the story of Abraham and his wife, Sarah. At the beginning of when we read about Abraham in Genesis chapter 12, we see that God promised Abraham that he would be a father to many nations. Except, Abraham and Sarah were very old, well beyond the age anyone conceived a child. Throughout the course of their marriage, Abraham and Sarah struggled with infertility, yet God continually reminded them of his promise to give them a child. Their patience wasn't easy, and required a lot of faith. Finally, when Abraham was one hundred and Sarah was ninety, they conceived and bore a son who they named Isaac. God kept his promise, even if it didn't happen the way or in the timeline Abraham and Sarah probably had expected.

There is an obvious running theme in these stories; God has a perfect track record of faithfulness. He has an immaculate record of keeping his promises.

As you're reading this, you might be wondering "what does this mean for me?" Unless you have had a divine encounter where the Holy Spirit has revealed a specific promise to you, you might be asking what God has promised you. I have good news. When you give your life to Jesus and surrender your will and desires to his, he promises you good things too. He promises you in Romans 8:28 that he is working all things together for the good of those who love him. He promises you in Jeremiah 29:11 that he has a perfect plan for your life, even if it's not immediate and you don't know what it is quite yet. God reminds you in Psalm 139 of your worth, your intricacy that started in the womb, and that you were fearfully and wonderfully made.

The last thing I want you to do is read this chapter and think that God promises that patience will always bring you a relationship. I want you to read this chapter and be reminded of the fact that no matter what your relationship status is, no matter if it ever changes, and whatever your past holds, that God keeps his promises. He is working all things together. He does have a plan and you do have a beautiful purpose even if that purpose doesn't mean having a ring on your finger.

I struggle with impatience a lot. I get antsy and on edge when things aren't going exactly how I want them or happening exactly as fast as I wanted them to. I have spent the last several years of my life learning to surrender my impatience, my plans, and my timeline to Jesus. I have spent hours of planning and dreaming and at the end of the day, if my heart isn't aligned with God's, then those desires and dreams are empty. Friend, when you fall in love with Jesus, when you really start praying that your heart's desires are tuned in with what he desires for you, your focus shifts, and your heart changes. That is the beauty of the Gospel.

So, how do you go about fighting the battle of impatience and discontentment specifically when it comes to your relationship status? How do you rest in the fact that we serve a God that knows what's best for us and remain faithfully patient in that? I don't have all of the answers, but I can share with you a few things that I have found that make it easier for me to remain patient in the Lord's timing.

1. You must stay grounded in his word.
   This is vital in your life, period, as a believer. But when you are working to grow in bearing the fruits of the spirit—in this case, patience—knowing the character of God is so incredibly important. The closer you hide his word in your heart, the easier it is to implement in your life.
2. Prioritize being plugged into biblical community.
   Biblical community allows you to live transparently and openly in the sin you are struggling with. Bringing struggles to the light allows you to make room for whatever is needed to work through those struggles. Whether this looks like accountability, hard heart checks, or just someone to confess to.
3. Practice having a heart posture of gratitude.
   Impatience in your current season stems from one of a few things: comparing your season to someone else's, unmet expectations, or being discontent individually with Jesus. No matter what underlying thing that your impatience is stemming from, gratitude can make a huge difference in shifting the posture of your heart. When we pivot our focus from the things we don't have, or the things we haven't done, to the things and experiences that we have been blessed with, it becomes a lot harder to meditate on the former. I challenge you, on days or moments when you feel especially impatient, to take a few minutes and genuinely thank God for a few things in your life that he has blessed you with, big or small.

You may be like, "Duh, Lauren; I know to do these things." But friend, I tell you this with the most loving yet firm resolve. Most Christians do not practice these things in ways that are a part of their lifestyle and routine. When we truly walk the walk, we adhere to the things that God gives us to live a life inside of his will, and become slower to grow impatient. Impatience leads to misery, and a life feeling miserable is the last thing God wants for you. And let me remind you, desiring a relationship is one thing, idolizing it is another. When we have a heart of impatience towards our love life, it is stemming from an idolatrous heart. Because when Jesus sits on the throne of our hearts, we are fully satisfied in him. Sound familiar from chapter 2?

Friend, I am cheering you on. I know waiting stinks. It can feel like God is distant, does not care, or doesn't want to honor your desires. I can promise you that's not the case. Just like one of my favorite songs by Hillsong says;

"You're the God of seasons
And I'm just in the winter
If all I know of harvest
Is that it's worth my patience
Then if You're not done working
God I'm not done waiting. . ."

Your season is coming. Hold fast to God's Word. He is in your corner.

# 4

# Expectations vs. Reality

Have you ever seen the social media posts or memes that have two pictures, and one is described as expectations and the other one is reality? One of the most common ongoing examples of this phenomenon has to do with online shopping. This is seen when someone posts a picture from the company's website of something they ordered, and then the actual product they receive when it comes in the mail. Nine times out of ten, the product will not live up to the buyer's standards, or expectations. The dress will be half the size it was supposed to be, the top will be a different color, or the shoes will be fake.

Another time I have seen this portrayed is the comparison of what a fast food hamburger may look like on commercials versus when it actually served to customers at the restaurant. It is *never* as appealing as the pictures and advertisements on TV, is it?

I feel like relationships can be a lot like this. All too often, we go into them expecting something completely different from the actual reality of what we will be experiencing. The world has given us this false reality of what relationships are like. This leads to unmet expectations, which in turn leads to failed relationships and broken hearts.

One of the best examples of how the world taints our views on relationships is through media and entertainment. Whether it be through reality TV, movies, social media influencers, or viral

YouTube videos, we are consistently being fed so many lies surrounding the idea of relationships.

I will admit, a guilty pleasure of mine for years now has been watching television shows produced by The Bachelor franchise. I know—controversial—but I have always enjoyed watching strangers's journeys to find love on national television. If you have not already been able to tell, I am a complete mush, a hopeless romantic to say the least. This may play a role in why I have always loved watching shows like this but nonetheless, these productions are prime examples of the "expectations versus reality" culture that we live in. If you have ever watched any of these shows, it is easy to dote over the seemingly heartfelt dates, extravagant activities, and all-around fairytale-like scenery and events that take place within these people's relationships.

In a normal season of The Bachelor, you will see the contestants fly all over the world to date each other in picturesque locations. From Bora Bora, to Thailand, and everywhere in between, these dates are once in a lifetime, and frankly, not realistic for 99 percent of the average human population. These atmospheres are specifically catered to aid in the process of falling in love. I mean, if you were riding in a hot air balloon over the Scottish plains with a beautiful, single human, you may agree that it would not be the hardest thing to fall in love under the circumstances. However, out of thirty-eight seasons of the main shows of this franchise, where almost all of them ended in an engagement and marriage, less than ten couples remain together today.

Why am I telling you this? Why is it important to this topic?

Because the world paints relationships in a starkly contrasted way compared to what the true reality is.

After the cameras turned off, regular clothes were put back on. Less glamorous tasks like laundry and dishes had to actually get done. The perfected version of these individuals with fancy wardrobes, perfectly made up faces, and styled hair broadcasted on television fizzled away and were replaced by real, messy humans with flaws and imperfections. When they found themselves in their everyday lives, these couples didn't last.

Now, one can speculate as to the specific reasons behind this, but I would attribute it to the way this franchise strives to manufacture a fairytale love story that sounds dreamy and perfect using two humans who are anything but. Where the "honeymoon phase" is all they know, which causes them to lose desire when real life starts to happen.

Yes, the comparison to shows such as The Bachelor may be a little extreme, but let me level with you. How many couples have you seen on social media or YouTube that seem to always be on cute dates? Or traveling the world together? Have you ever stopped to think that those couples have finances to worry about too? That they fight, argue, and have hard days too?

If you haven't, that is a prime example of how easy it is to live in an "expectations versus reality" clouded world.

The truth is, friend, relationships are messy. They are hard. They are made up of two broken humans. Humans that have flaws, that were born into sinful human nature just like the rest of us. And despite what you may believe, the union of two sinners does not equal a lack of sin, or an easy fix; it doubles the sin and brokenness.

We read in Galatians 6 that we are to bear each other's burdens, and that is what biblical relationships look like: taking on each other's burdens as our own.

Biblical relationships and marriages are beautiful, don't get me wrong. But at the end of the day, biblical marriage is the commitment to a lifelong journey with another sinner. A life that—as we are told in Scripture—*will* have hardship and pain.

Not only can false expectations lead us to be let down in relationships, but they can also lead us to harm our partner in the process.

Expectations lead to comparison. They lead to us being robbed of our joy and ability to see the beauty in the circumstance God has us in. The presence of expectations clouds the beauty God has intended for relationships to bring when done for the glory of Him.

I have personally experienced this struggle in my own relationships. In some cases, it was a situation where I did not have realistic expectations, and that led to being let down because of the reality I faced. And in other cases, it was because I felt my expectations were valid, but I never communicated them with the other person, which put them in an unfair spot of not being able to fulfill the expectations I had.

All in all, expectations have the potential to be brutal to your emotional wellbeing, your partner's emotional wellbeing, and the overall wellbeing of your relationship.

When you have unrealistically high expectations for a relationship, it is easy to neglect the fact that Jesus is our only constant in this life. Even when you have found a spouse and are in a Godly marriage, you are still married to an equally broken person. A person that will mess up, hurt you, fail, and neglect to meet your expectations all of the time. This is why it is vital for us to cling to Jesus with all that we have, for he is our only consistent source of not only met but often surpassed expectations in this life here on earth.

Remembering these things is so important, especially when you find yourself struggling with comparison, or impatience while waiting for a relationship to come your way in the midst of singleness. When our attention is centered around Pinterest quotes and Instagram-able date nights, the desire for a relationship rules over us even more, when in reality, we are hoping for something that is not possible. Because it's not realistic 100 percent of the time.

The world feeds us the lies of couple's traveling to exotic vacations all the time, where every date night involves cute picnic baskets and string lights, where flirting is the norm, and fighting is nowhere in sight. We are fed the false reality that once you find your person, it is smooth sailing from there on out.

The things we are fed by the world miss the parts like how a dream house isn't something that just happens overnight but takes years of hard labor and planning, or traveling together takes a lot of budgeting. Many times, date nights look like fast food or grocery store trips. One of you might have a hard diagnosis at some point.

We miss the part where biblical relationships look like choosing love over feelings and receiving gratification most of the time. Seeking Christ in relationships requires us to die to ourselves and our own desires every single day. Christ-honoring relationships are free of expectations and full of grace and imperfection made perfect because of Christ's love for us.

At the end of the day, our earthly relationships are intended to reflect the relationship our Heavenly Father has with his church. A sacrificial, servant-hearted, selfless, unconditional, "I would give up my life for you" type of love.

This is the reality of biblical relationships.

To help you reflect on this chapter, I have prayed over and put together some prompts for you to ponder and reflect on yourself. This can be done with someone else, or alone. God's desire for you is to live a life that reflects his love, even in relationships. It's messy, broken, imperfect, but even more so, it is a beautiful reflection of the redemption we have in Jesus.

Prompts:

*"When have I let my own expectations cloud reality?"*

*"Have my expectations ever led to the harm of another person's heart?"*

For those in a relationship:

*"How can I rid myself of expectations and cling to the grace of Jesus in my relationship?"*

For those who are single:

*"After really reflecting on the reality of what relationships truly look like in a Biblical context, am I ready for that? How can I prepare my heart now to not bring in any false expectations to my future relationship?"*

# 5

# How Far Is Too Far?

If you have ever been a Christian in a dating relationship, or even paid attention to Christians who are in relationships, you have most definitely heard or asked this question before: "How far is too far?"

Guilty as charged.

It's a hot button issue because purity culture and boundaries in relationships while following Jesus have become a huge deal in society. I would go as far as to say that it has become an idol, but that is an issue for another day, or chapter.

We see a lot of questions like: Is premarital kissing okay? What about making out? Can we cuddle or lay down together? How about spending the night together with no sex?

These are often met with people trying to make up a cut and dry list of physical relational boundaries that—news flash—are nowhere to be found in the Bible. Yep, I just said that.

There are some areas in Christianity that we don't have a set of commandments or literal rules to follow, and this is one of them. Now, hear me right, 1 Corinthians 7:1-2 makes it clear that the one thing we do know is that premarital sex is a sin, end of story, hard stop, period. But all of the little things leading up to sex? We have to discern and decide for ourselves. Thus, leading to the question: "How far is too far?"

Full disclosure here, I am an extremely physical person. Physical touch ranks as my second love language and if I ever have the pleasure of meeting you in person, I will most definitely give you a hug. You know, if we aren't in a pandemic or anything.

With that being said, as someone who receives love well through physical touch, and in return, gives it in that way, I found myself really struggling with this question when I was a teenager entering the dating world.

I say I struggled with it, because it truly is a gray area like I mentioned before. When you enter into a relationship, you probably will, or at least should, find yourself reassessing this issue multiple times pre-marriage. I watched a ton of videos on YouTube, read many blogs, and listened to countless sermons in hopes of finding some concrete answer to this prevailing question.

Truthfully, I am a grade A rule follower, and a coined "goody two shoes" by all of my middle school classmates, so I needed a set of rules. A guidebook, a list of do's and don'ts.

But despite all my searching, I never did find a black and white answer.

Gray issues in the Bible are something I really wrestle with. I've come to define them as "issues or topics that God gives us free will to discern our own convictions through the eyes of the Gospel and Scripture."

That last tidbit, "through the eyes of the Gospel and Scripture," is the vital part there, because I don't want you to think that we have free reign to pick parts of the Bible we want to follow while neglecting the others. This is not me saying that premarital sex is okay for some while it isn't for others, and it is up to you to decide. No, because we have set rules for that.

I am talking about things like kissing, cuddling, hugging, making out, tongue or no tongue (uncomfortable, I know, but I promised transparency), and traveling together.

These are all things that God did not give us a list of boundary commandments in the Bible. It took me a long time wrestling with this to actually realize the beauty in God allowing us to discern things for ourselves. The free will he gives us is an opportunity to grow closer to him, hold fast to him, and truly increase in intimacy with the Father.

Before I continue, I want to throw in a little disclaimer that with discussing gray areas comes the fact that everything that works for me, or that I have implemented in my dating life, might not work well for you. I will explain more thoroughly in a moment. But the last thing I want you to take away from this chapter is that I am giving you a specific set of rules or boundaries to live by, because that is not what I am trying to do. Rather, I want to show you how I have gone on the journey of discerning for myself, and give you tools to be able to use so you can do the same.

While the Bible does not have verses that say whether or not to kiss or cuddle, there is plenty of Scripture that we can apply to our question of how far is too far.

Many Christians have the wrong idea, because they pay attention to the no premarital sex part, but take it and run with it while proceeding to teeter very close to the line of doing everything *but* engage in actual intercourse. This is not the way God intended.

To start, there are some understandings I want to establish because they are very foundational to see how God intended sex. He designed sex to be something beautiful and a precious gift to humanity, but only to be received in marriage. He designed it as a way married couples can not only grow in intimacy with each other, but intimacy with Jesus, as it is an act of sacred worship when done in the confines that God made it for: marriage.

God is intentional and all knowing when he gives us any boundary or rule; therefore, I don't believe he is trying to make life less fun or pleasurable by commanding us to wait until marriage to engage in sex. But rather, I believe he is intentional in the ways he intends for us to guard our hearts to only experience that level of intimacy with someone we have a covenant with for the rest of our lives. I believe that the parameters he gives us in all aspects of life, including sex, are not to confine or restrain us, but rather to free and liberate us to be able to enjoy all of his beauty the way he created us to.

Matthew 5:6 tells us that those who strive and hunger for righteousness are blessed. This is a call to strive for holiness and closeness to Jesus above all else.

Meaning, not only are we told to not have sex before marriage, but in that, we are to flee from sexual immorality while striving for holiness. It is way more than a line that can't be crossed.

The question "How far is too far?" is not an issue of how close we can get to the line without crossing it, but a matter of how far can we stay away from it in order to bring glory to Jesus and the template he so beautifully crafted for relationships to model. If we are viewing it as any other way but the latter, we have it all wrong. Jesus not only tells us to not engage in sexual immorality, but it is the one sin he actually tells us to *flee* from. I don't know about you, but when I picture fleeing from something, I picture running away from it as fast as I can, trying my hardest not to get anywhere near it. That is why teetering on the line isn't the answer, but holding fast to Jesus while staying far away from the line is.

Like I said before, this was something I struggled with for a while, but my mindset really shifted when the rhetoric in my mind changed from "How far can I go physically with the person I am dating?" to "How much can I honor my future husband by saving as much as I can for him and only him?"

This is where my heart shifted, and I began to truly see the beauty that comes with boundaries. I began to rejoice in the fact that the God we serve not only wants us to honor and glorify him with our bodies and relationships, but he desires for us to be protected from hurt, shame, and guilt. The way we view God when it relates to boundaries is vital if we want to set healthy ones. When we change our mindset from thinking that he is trying to keep us from something good to the reality that He is actually just preparing us for something better, we can truly live freely and begin to set intentional boundaries in relationships.

I once heard an analogy in regard to this topic during a sermon. The pastor was talking about picturing a beautiful house with a big, lush, green yard, and surrounding it was a white picket fence. He went on to explain how when we see a house like this with a fence around the perimeter of the land, we don't immediately think to ourselves that the homeowners are being mean by not letting trespassers get to their house. No, we see it as a gate that is surrounding a beautiful piece of property that the house is centered in. You don't see anyone with a fence up against the bricks of their house, because they are not just trying to keep you from the actual house, but the area surrounding it.

We can use this analogy to look at our sexual purity, with our purity being the house in the middle of the fenced-in land, and the white picket fence being the boundaries we have discerned and set for ourselves. Remember: God is not trying to keep anything good from you, He is simply saving and preparing you for something much better.

Now, I know you may be super aggravated because you were expecting me to give you a set list of rules and boundaries I followed, but I am not going to do that. However, what I will do is let you in on how I discerned my own personal boundaries and the process in which I established the answer to the question "How far is too far?" for myself.

One of the ways that I used to evaluate a boundary was with a triangle analogy. The two bottom points represent me and my significant other, and the top point represents Jesus. The goal for all of your romantic relationships if you are a Christian, should be to grow closer and closer to God each day in your relationship. This can be shown through the triangle picture because as you two are getting closer together, you are also growing closer towards Jesus.

If I ever questioned something in regards to boundaries, I would always ask myself: "Is engaging in this act going to lead me closer to Jesus with my significant other?" If the answer was no, I would normally take that as a way of knowing I needed to set up a boundary.

Another practical way of deciphering which boundaries you need to have in place is to simply have a (potentially uncomfortable but very worth it) conversation with your boyfriend or girlfriend. I would recommend day two of your dating relationship at the latest—this allows no room for questioning or opportunity to cross a line you have yet to set. This conversation will probably be one that you have to have a few times, because relationships and feelings change. Naturally, as you grow more in love with someone, you are going to desire more of them physically, but in order to not let lust cloud your vision, you may need to reevaluate if you feel you are crossing a line.

Someone once told me that if your body is preparing for sex, then you have gone too far. And that answers a lot of questions right there.

It is also important to remember that boundaries look different from person to person. For some couples, holding hands is too far, while for others it may not bother them at all. Also, your partner may have stricter boundaries than you, or vice versa. If that is the case, go with whoever has the stronger convictions, so you don't cause the other person to stumble. This may feel unfair, but remember—the point of a relationship that's working to potentially end in marriage is to reflect the sacrificial love Jesus has for us.

It really is a case by case basis, which is why you will not find a set list from me.

Here are some questions to ask yourself or discuss with your significant other when establishing and evaluating boundaries:

1. Have we lusted after one another in our minds or hearts?
2. Have we gone so far as to a point where we feel like we can't stop?
3. Are we putting ourselves in positions that make us easily vulnerable? (Alone in an empty house for example)
4. Do I feel any conviction when I ask the Holy Spirit to guide me in this way? Never underestimate the power of his still small voice.

Lastly, and I want to end on this note.

You are no less if you have crossed a line.

You are not damaged goods if you have had premarital sex.

You are worthy regardless of the lengths to which you have gone physically.

You are not less pure if you have been violated in any way. And if you have, I am so sorry. I won't act like I know what you have experienced, but I do know that God views you all the same, and what happened was not your fault.

There is redemption and power in the grace of the Gospel.

I have met and talked to so many girls who have crossed a boundary and feel like there is no point in reestablishing them or saving themselves for their future spouse because they feel like they are too far gone. Friend, that statement could not be further from the truth. If you have been told that lie, I am here to tell you that that is not the Gospel. The Gospel is not works-based, but is through grace and grace alone.

It is never too late to prioritize purity or recommit to that. When you come to Jesus with a heart of conviction and willingness to submit to his will, he makes you pure again and has already forgiven you a million times over.

All too often people treat sexual purity as the one sin God cannot redeem you of, but our God is a God of redemption and unconditional love and forgiveness, period.

I hope this chapter gave you a glimpse into my heart behind boundaries, and that you are moving on feeling empowered and freed in the Gospel. You are so loved. Your identity is not in the things of this world.

# 6

# It's Not Just Physical

I thought that this chapter would be perfect to follow the boundaries topic because I briefly expounded upon my "why" in the last chapter, but this time I'd like to go even deeper. The argument I hear by far the most in regard to physical affection is "What's the matter with (fill in the blank)? It's just physical. . ." This argument is honestly not valid, and I want to lovingly share with you why this outlook towards physical affection is so wrong, and honestly, quite devastating.

It's the people who have this mindset that end up with more guilt, shame, regret, and heartache when they enter into their marriages. It's the people that wish that they could do something, anything, to get back a piece of their heart from a past lover.

Now I do not want you to think that the purpose of this chapter is to go all anti-affection on you, because trust me, my number one love language is physical affection. I understand the desire to be intimate, to be affectionate, to physically love someone you are in a romantic relationship with. What I want to do is simply share a perspective that helps shed a different Christ-like light on this topic. Because not only is this a topic that is not talked about in the church, but it is also looked down upon and considered shameful to even bring up. In my opinion, the worst way we, as Christians, can approach any hard topic in life, is to not talk about it at all. On an issue where darkness is so prevalent, we need to do better at shining light on it through a Kingdom lens. I know so many teenagers who would have loved for their pastors or youth groups to answer these hard questions, but never heard a biblical perspective on it before they were thrown into the sinful way our world views sex and affection.

This is something that truly breaks my heart, because it shakes me to my core that we have generation Z being looked down upon and ridiculed because of the way we handle ourselves in relationships. How are we supposed to act in relationships through a Christlike lens if our own church leaders won't answer our questions or address the hard issues? It's kind of like when a Christian gets mad at a nonbeliever for doing something that, apart from Jesus, they wouldn't know is wrong. It is unfair to judge a nonbeliever or expect them to act a certain way that they would if they had a relationship with Jesus, because the reality is that they don't.

One of the biggest ways that I think the American church has done us a disservice is how it narrates attraction and desire. Within Christian circles, we tend to treat desire as something that is wrong, dirty, and sinful. We tell young teens that being attracted to someone in a physical way is bad, which often leads to them resorting to pornography and masturbation behind closed doors because they feel ashamed.

Friend, desire is not a sin. Attraction is not a sin. God created us to be in relationship with him *and* others. He created us to see the beauty in others as a reflection of him. God could have made marriage boring by not giving us attraction but instead he created us with desires so that we may experience the beautiful gift he has given us through relationships.

I think that debunking this lie is one of the first steps that our generation needs to start pursuing and desiring Godly relationships. What if we changed the narrative? I feel sure that not as many teens and young adults would resort to pornography out of curiosity if they actually felt safe asking questions to a trusted adult who follows Jesus. And to the parents or adults who may read this, do we not want the younger generation to hear these things through a Kingdom-oriented lens? Yes, I know it is more than uncomfortable, but what is more important? Your child viewing sex and relationships through a biblical lens or your comfort that leads them to go ask questions and find answers elsewhere, in a place far from scriptural truth? These are hard issues, but they are also real issues. Ones that need reviving and rewriting.

With that being said, I hope to be a small part of teaching or reminding you of the way God made us to enjoy relationships in a way that reflects his love for us.

I remember when I was in one of my first ever serious relationships in high school, I began to struggle with the idea of what the importance behind a kiss truly was. I know, it may seem silly, but I went through phases where I was determined to save my first kiss for my fiancé or husband, and then other times where I had a mindset that it was just a kiss, it didn't mean much. It was only when I reached out to one of my mentors that things sort of clicked. She explained that even though a kiss may seem super small in the big picture, the reason it matters so much is because regardless of the kiss, that is still an intimate part of you and an intimate moment you will forever share with the other person. No matter how small, or big, you are sharing a deeply personal part of yourself through engaging in something such as a kiss with them.

I still had some questions after processing it, and wondered, "How am I giving a piece of myself away through kissing them?" She explained that if I went around kissing everyone I dated or was attracted to, it would surely affect my future relationship with my spouse when we had to have that conversation about our relational history. How would he feel if he found out that I kissed a whole bunch of guys before him? He might question the value I place on myself and physical intimacy.

I truly believe that the value and worth that we believe that we have as individuals has a direct effect on how we go about relationships. If I value myself, and know that I am a daughter of the one true King, and I know that my body is his, would it change the way I interact physically with the opposite sex? I think so, without a doubt. If you place little to no value on yourself and your body, and more importantly, who Jesus says you are, who's to say you can't just go sleep with everyone you meet because it truly doesn't matter?

Do you see what I am getting at?

When we evaluate physical affection, we have to delve deep into our own worth and how we view ourselves, because it trickles into every other aspect of our lives. Your body belongs to Jesus, and is a temple, a dwelling place for the Holy Spirit. You are valuable and worthy, because Christ deemed you those things through his Son dying on the cross for you.

This is why boundaries are important. This is why it is so much more than just physical.

Every time we give parts of our affection and body to a significant other, we are giving a little piece of our hearts away. While it may be small, it is still a piece. I don't want to scare or discourage you, but it's true. It's a hard reality to digest. Every breakup I've had where I have kissed the person, I always wish I could get that back so that I could save it for my person.

And while I know that saving all of your physical affection only for your future spouse is not exactly important and feasible for everyone, it truly is something to think about when establishing boundaries in future relationships. You have to think big picture, and also, not only just about your future spouse, but about yourself. Because you are worthy of being fully known and loved too. God has equipped you with his Spirit to have self-control and discernment so that you may not give too much of your heart away, which could lead to hurt and heartbreak.

I tell you all of these things as a sister in Christ, not to condemn you, but to equip you to be able to set yourself up for the most joy, peace, and love possible.

The way we see relationships and physicality truly does change when we establish and analyze our worth from the cross. Jesus changes everything, even this area of your life. And if you are struggling to see where I am coming from when I say these things, or if I have freaked you out at all, I encourage you to take it to Jesus. Seek him out, pray for your heart to desire the things that he desires for you.

And don't feel ashamed if you struggle with these things, or sin in these areas of life.

Let me remind you, God created our bodies. He created sex. He created attraction.

These are good things, beautiful things, but they also mean so much to God that we need to look to him for wisdom when we have questions or confusion.

Some arguments I have heard towards the fact that Christians don't engage in premarital sex are that "Our world is different now," or "That isn't relevant anymore." And what I would pose in return is, if you truly believe in God, in the fact that he created us fully, then why would you disregard what he tells us to do—or not do—with our bodies? He did give them to us, after all. He wired us to be the way we are, and that is relevant and timeless. God is the same yesterday, today, and forever. The same can be said of his Word and his will.

Like I mentioned in the last chapter, God does not intend for us to view boundaries as something that holds us back, restricts us, or deprives us of pleasure. Rather, he wants us to truly see that he is saving and preparing us for something better. I will you tell you from personal conversation I have had with married adults in my life, married sex is better than any other type of sex outside of wedlock. Jesus has our best in mind. And yes, it takes patience, self-control, and perseverance, but it is worth it to be able to experience physical affection in all of its fullness as God intended us to.

To end this chapter, I want to give you some questions to ponder and pray about if you or someone you know has ever struggled with this issue. Trust me, I have, and it is not easy. I also want to leave you with the encouragement that God made us to desire one another, and you are not dirty because of that, nor are you alone in that.

I also want to remind you of the importance of community. When we have community, we have people who love us and want to hold us accountable. When I was beginning to date, I let a few of my closest Christian friends and mentors know exactly what boundaries I had set in place for my significant other and me so that they could hold me accountable to those specific things. Sometimes that looked like them texting me at a certain time of night to make sure

I wasn't alone with the other person, or weekly check-ins to make sure my intentions were pure that week.

There is no shame in asking for help and counsel. In fact, God encourages and commands us to be in a community that helps remind us to keep our gaze fixed on him. Proverbs 15:22 tells us: "Plans fail for lack of counsel, but with many advisors they succeed."

We were never meant to do life alone.

I know this was a weighty chapter, but I promise it comes out of my love and desire for you to live a dating life that pleases and honors God.

Some questions you can ask yourself:

1. What do I believe about myself and the value and worth that I hold?
2. Do I believe any lies in regard to how I view myself?
3. If so, how has that impacted my view of physical boundaries and attraction?
4. Do I need to reevaluate the boundaries I have set in place with my significant other? Your answer may be yes if you find yourself lusting after them or crossing boundaries you have already set.
5. Do I have someone close to me who is a Christ follower and can hold me accountable in this area of life?

I hope this gave you some practical things you can apply in your romantic life, I know it may have been a lot to digest, so bear with me. You made it through chapter six! I am so proud of you for seeking purity and desiring Jesus in some of the most uncomfortable areas of life.

# 7

# For the Girls: Submission

Do you remember at youth group retreats when it would get to the part of the weekend where they would split up the girls and guys to talk about things that you, as a middle schooler, were not mature enough to hear around the opposite sex? If you read my first book, you will probably recognize the format of the next couple of chapters. For this chapter, I am going to bring you back to youth group for a second and separate the girls from the guys.

This chapter is specifically for my girls but I want to actually encourage guys to read through this chapter and likewise for girls in regard to the chapter on guys coming up next. However, I will go ahead and say that you may have to get into a different head space because this chapter will specifically be written towards girls and applicable to girls and not guys specifically. But for the guys that may be reading this, you will definitely gain some insight as to how to love your future wife, and vice versa for your future husbands on the next chapter, girls. Which leads me to mention, the Scripture passage I will be diving into is speaking specifically to husbands and wives. This is not for boyfriends and girlfriends, this is not for your male friend or your boss. These statements and confines are specifically meant to be taken to heart within the covenant of Christian marriage.

In essence, regardless of your gender, read through the next couple of chapters with the audience in mind. I want to challenge you to rid yourself of all that culture has said about this topic, all of the negative connotations surrounding this. Instead I invite you to pray and ask God to give you Kingdom vision only so that you may see this topic through his lens of love and grace.

The widely known excerpt and reference that we think of on women's calling to submit, and men's calling to lead, is in Ephesians 5:22–28.

> Wives, submit to your husbands as to the Lord, because the husband is the head of the wife as Christ is the head of the church. He is the Savior of the body. Now as the church submits to Christ, so also wives are to submit to their husbands in everything. Husbands, love your wives, just as Christ loved the church and gave himself for her to make her holy, cleansing her with the washing of water by the word. He did this to present the church to himself in splendor, without spot or wrinkle or anything like that, but holy and blameless. In the same way, husbands are to love their wives as their own bodies. He who loves his wife loves himself.

Yep. *That* passage.

You are most likely in one of two camps right now: you have never heard this passage be preached about, or you have but it was done in a way that dismissed the responsibility of the man and idolized the idea of a submissive, modest, doormat wife.

This is because hard topics are uncomfortable to talk about, and in the American church we have a very hard time putting our comfort idols to the side to make room for Jesus.

I don't know about you, but I would much rather be *in* God's will and *outside* of my comfort zone, than *outside* of his will but *in* my comfort zone.

I know that submission is a touchy subject, and one that isn't talked about hardly at all, but it's necessary. And that in and of itself is my heart behind talking about the hard things such as women submitting to their husbands. I have no ill intent, I have no desire to step on toes, but the reality is, the Gospel can be offensive. Because we are innately sinful but we were intended to be in communion with Jesus. Therefore, things that go against our nature may offend us, but they are necessary to realize if our desire is to fulfill the calling that God has for us and our relationships.

First off, I want to debunk some of the biggest lies that accompany this passage when we take it out of context and take Gospel-centered masculinity and femininity out of the picture. Rather than sharing the lies specifically, here are the truths that counteract them, and you can easily figure out what the lies that attempt to distract us from these beautiful truths are:

1. Men and women are equal, but they have different roles.
2. Men and women have different roles, but they are complementary to each other within God's design of marriage.
3. Because they are complementary to each other, we, as people and as a society, need them both equally to walk in their God-given calling. We do not need one more than the other, because God does not value one more than the other.
4. Both men *and* women's roles can be abused, and when abused, be harmful to those around them.

I want to expound upon these four different points individually so that we can be on the same page. And in this chapter, I am going to speak directly to women in light of these points, and will do the exact same for guys in the next chapter.

Women:

Although society may have taken this verse out of context to your detriment, you and your roles have no less or more value than those of your male counterpart. You are needed just as much as a man is. However, your role is different than a man within a marriage, and when you try to take the role of a man into your own hands, it is just as damaging as a man taking his role and abusing it.

In order to grasp this concept as much as we can, we have to go back to the origins of marriage with Adam and Eve in the very beginning.

Marriage is a phenomenon that can be described as a "cultural universal," meaning that no matter where you go in the world, marriage exists in some capacity. No matter how poor, rich, big, or small a culture is, marriage is present. With this being said, remember how a few chapters ago, I mentioned how there are a few gray areas in Christianity? You will be happy to hear that marriage is not one of those.

And all of the type-A personalities said "amen."

God makes a huge deal about marriage and he talks a lot about it. He gives us a list of extensive boundaries and guidelines in regard to marriage, which shows us just how big God's heart is for the marriage covenant. One of the most interesting things that I love to mention when talking about biblical marriage is how the Bible literally begins and ends with marriage.

It begins with marriage in that of Genesis when God made man, Adam, and then said "It is not good for man to be alone," which in turn led him to create woman, Eve. In Genesis 1:24 we see where the two become one flesh, the same phrase we see when God reiterates the purpose of marriage later in Scripture. The Bible ends with marriage in Revelation 19:7 when the "wedding of the Lamb has come," meaning the reuniting of Jesus and his bride, the church.

If this doesn't show how much value God places on the marriage covenant I don't know what does. The reason this is so important to understand is because marriage serves a greater purpose than any other relationship because it demonstrates the union between God and his children. This is why it is vital for us to truly grasp the difference and intention of the different roles God gives husbands and wives in marriage.

In Genesis 2:18, you read where God talks about how it is not good for Adam to be alone, and his intent behind creating Eve for Adam. His exact words are "*I will make a helper fit for him.*" In my own personal experience, us women seem to get kind of offended when reading this verse, because we interpret it as "we're *just* the help" and we belittle the actual meaning of this verse. This word "*help*" translates to the Hebrew word "*ezer,*" and is used in other Scripture such as Psalm 33:20 to describe God to us; our *help,* or our *ezer.*

How incredibly beautiful is that!

The same word that God used to describe the reason he created woman for man is also used to describe God to David in his time of need in Psalms. The word "helper" is not a belittling word, but rather an empowering one when we learn the true meaning and origins behind it. Adam was given a calling, and Eve was created to come alongside him to help fulfill this calling.

Just because men and women have different roles does not mean that one role is superior over the other. One of the many beauties of marriage is how impeccably it shows equality with distinction—a concept our modern-day society struggles to grasp.

When we look at Biblical marriage and see how the man is commanded to lead while the woman is commanded to submit, our mind immediately goes into a mode of insecurity and defensiveness because of the way our culture has influenced our view of marriage and roles. My goal for this chapter and the next is to lovingly explain with conviction how we have gotten it all wrong, and why submission and leadership is not only a command, but a good and beautiful thing to walk in as a woman.

So, with all of that being said, we'll be going back to the four aforementioned truths that apply to this passage and this concept of submission and leadership. My goal is to walk through each one of them and illustrate how they bring the truth of the Gospel and Gospel-centered marriage.

To expound upon the first and second points, men and women are equal, but have different roles. The lie that men and women are not equal because they have very different roles is one of the most harmful beliefs that our society can adopt. I can't begin to fathom how many more relationships would be prosperous, marriages would be saved, and conflicts would be avoided if we were able to remember and live out this simple truth.

We are so prone to assume that because in Scripture, God gives the responsibility of the man to lead in relationships, that women are automatically inferior. This just isn't true. I like to think of the Trinity, the three-in-one God we serve consisting of the Father, Son, and Holy Spirit. All characteristics of the Trinity have different roles in our faith life but all of them are essential and contribute to the beauty and fullness of God in our lives. The Holy Spirit exists to live within us and dwell in our hearts so that we can discern and follow his call. The Father gave up Jesus, his Son, so that the salvation that Jesus embodies can give to us eternal life. All different roles, all divinely beautiful and necessary. In marriage, man and woman have different roles, but ones that make up the Gospel-representing union of marriage and ones that cannot exist exclusive to one another.

The third point mentions the truth of how because the roles within marriage are complementary, and exist to fulfill a shared calling, God does not value one more than the other, and this is empowering for women and men alike. Women, your role is not more or less important in marriage in comparison to your husband. This is true for him as well.

Lastly, and probably the truth that I feel is the most important to remind you of, is how both men and women can abuse their roles in relationships. Oftentimes, we automatically assume that if a Christian relationship is unhealthy, that it's because of the man abusing his roles and responsibilities. This makes me sad, because we, as women, have equal responsibility to sustain our roles in our relationships in a Godly way. It is doing such a disservice to the men in our lives if we immediately assume that a lacking in their roles are the main causes of downfalls in relationships. A woman that is not submitting to her husband, speaking into him, or respecting and honoring him is just as harmful as a guy who is not leading his wife well. This all goes back to the beautiful truth that our gender-specific roles in marriage are equal and just as valuable as our male counterpart. This is motivation for us women to do our parts in lifting up our husbands in a way that edifies, and strengthens them in the Lord.

We see this phenomenon in Scripture in the very beginning in Genesis when the fall of man happens. How many times have you jokingly blamed the start of sin and fall of humanity on Eve because she's the one who ate the forbidden fruit? Yeah, me too. It wasn't until diving into Scripture with the purpose of studying to write this book that I realized that Adam and Eve were equally at fault in this situation. Because Adam decided to let apathy and passivity overtake him in this instant where he should have been leading his wife, Eve decided to take control and that resulted in what happened next. Adam had a responsibility, and the root of the sin that led to her eating the fruit, actually began with him not walking in biblical leadership. The command to not eat of that tree in the garden was originally given to Adam, and there, in that moment, Eve was leading Adam because he neglected to lead her.

This is a perfect representation of how the roles that we may dub as societally "more important" are equally as vital to the relationships we foster.

Now, with the hard concept of submission, us girls have to understand what biblical femininity truly looks like. Because apart from that, submission has no place. It is because of the women we are in the Lord that we can realize the purpose of submitting and everything that falls into our role as women.

Before I continue on what biblical femininity alone looks like, let's lay the groundwork. In saying biblical femininity, I am talking about what the Bible calls women to walk in to flourish. This is not about being a wife, mom, or sister—it's not about roles. It is about your identity as a flourishing woman of God. Another precursor that I want to reiterate is that men and women are created equal, but they carry different responsibilities and roles. Men and women are like puzzle pieces, different but complementary; fitting together to create a complete bigger picture.

In going through scripture and listening to a lot of wise counsel on this topic, I want to give you three things we know that women of God embody, and the lies society uses to distort those three things.

*The first truth: Women of the Lord have empowering strength.*

In Genesis 2:18, we see that word "helper," in Greek: *"ezer."* The word I mentioned earlier, that is issued sixteen other times in scripture to describe God himself. It translates to help, and to rescue. As women, when we walk in accordance with our Creator, we embody empowering strength; a powerful, corresponding, perfectly suited rescuer for the people around us.

*The distortion/lie: Codependency.*

This can look like women "needing to be needed," or someone relying too much on you, or the false urge to change or fix people. We have to hold fast to the truth that we are not the true rescuer, but we have the ability to point people to him; to Jesus. When walking in the God-given strength you have as a woman, submission doesn't have to be belittling, in fact it is part of what makes your strength empowering. There is immense power in submission; that of humility, trust, and grace.

*The second truth: Women of the Lord extend refuge.*

When we are walking with Jesus, we have the gift of being able to extend refuge to others. Sometimes that can be literal, but most often it comes with the gentle spirit that we have in Jesus to extend peace and calm to those around us. This does not mean we can never speak or use our voice, see truth number one. What this does mean, is that when you are so rooted in who God has made you to be and what Jesus has done to save you, you will spread that to others around you. I heard this analogy in a sermon one time about the difference in what this looks like between men and women in a tangible way. The pastor talked about how in a home, the men often resemble the four walls and the roof of the house; providing and protecting. And then he went on to explain how the woman resembles the couch and fireplace; what makes the house a home, cozy and welcoming. The way that you are able to extend refuge to others through the spirit in you as a woman is powerful, essential, and valuable.

*The distortion/lie: Anxiety and insecurity.*

When sin distorts this truth of your identity, insecurity spreads to everyone around you because you aren't finding your own security in God but in your surroundings. As women, this should spur us on to submit to the Lord so that others around us feel that overflow of his love.

*Third truth: Women of the Lord cultivate beauty.*

In 1 Peter 3:3-4, we see God's definition of beauty explained. We read that the beauty a woman beholds is not outward, but inward in spirit. Women were created in the image of God, and God is captivating, lovely, and beautiful. This beauty we radiate comes from him and is lasting, not fleeting, like external beauty. When women walk in this, beauty is cultivated around them, turning chaos into order, brokenness turned towards God's design.

Have you ever had a woman in your life who those around her would describe as the glue that holds her home together? I know I have. For me, that's the way my dad has always described my mom. Because of her Godly submission to Jesus, she cultivates beauty around her through the overflow of his beauty in her. Without her presence, our house would be a mess; and while this could be taken literally, I am referring to the spirit of the home. While it is true that she keeps our house in physical order, her first priority and gifting is helping to cultivate beauty in those living and coming into our home.

*The distortion/lie: Body image.*

This one is self-explanatory. So often us women get caught up in the outward beauty that society tells us is where our worth and value is found. We become focused on the number on the scale, or the brands we wear, or fill in the blank. By looking at what the Bible says about us, we know this beauty is meaningless, we know that God defines beauty as something completely different than how society would define it. And because what God says about us is the truest thing about us, we know we are beautiful because he says we are, and that beauty is inward.

After reading through this explanation on biblical femininity, I know the possibility is there that you could be super overwhelmed. That's valid, because as women, we have huge responsibilities, but here is the truth that can calm your unease:

You are not enough. You alone never have been and you never will be enough. But there is good news. Everything God invites you to be as a woman of the Lord, he was and is for you. He brought all sin and insecurity to the cross with him, and he embodies the things we can't be so that in him, we are enough to be the flourishing women he created us to be.

I hope that these words encouraged you, that they reminded you, or taught you more of what God says about who he created you to be. I hope it empowered you, and showed you that while your role is different than a man's, that it is just as important to God's design.

As you move onto the next chapter, where I talk about biblical masculinity and leadership, I encourage you to ponder these questions and prompts:

1. What lies have you believed about yourself if you're a woman, or if you aren't, the women around you, that you realized were false while reading through this chapter?
2. What can practical repentance look like in that? Do you need to apologize to a woman in your life? Do you need to rethink your role in the relationship you're in?
3. Lastly, for my girls reading this, how can you consistently remind yourself of the truths spoken over you in this chapter? Can you memorize some scripture? Perhaps write some of these truths on the face of a mirror you look into daily?

# 8

# For the Guys: Leadership

I will never forget a story I heard told in a sermon on biblical masculinity one Sunday at my church. The pastor that was preaching began to share how one time he had a student from church over for dinner, and his two younger sons, around five or six years old at the time, began to fight with each other. When the boys started to physically get rough with each other, he pulled them aside and said, "Boys, why did God give men strength?"

They sighed and responded, "To protect, help, and defend others."

The dad then asked, "What do we never use our strength to do?"

The two young boys sighed again and said "We never use our strength to hurt others." The student he had over for dinner began to sob and when the pastor asked what was wrong, he began to explain how different his life would be if he had ever had a man in his life teach him what he had instilled in his young sons.

I can't help but tear up every time I hear or am reminded of that story. It makes me really sit and ponder how different some circumstances in my own life would be had that been the narrative the men around me had realized growing up.

I wanted to begin with that story in this chapter, because as I begin to unpack what leadership looks like for a Godly man in a relationship, and ultimately biblical masculinity as a whole, I want you to remember that the ways our society shapes us are almost always at odds with the ways Scripture teaches us to live our lives. As scary and sad as this is, it is a fierce reminder that we are broken, but there is hope. We are sinners, but we are saved by grace through Jesus.

If you happen to be a guy reading this, and you didn't read the previous chapter where I was specifically talking to girls, I encourage you to go back and read it. However, if you choose not to, the thing I need to remind you of most importantly is despite the fact that your role is different than a woman's in a relationship; it is complementary and not inferior or superior to her role. God made men and women different, yet fully equal.

While most of this book pertains to romantic relationships, I want you to keep in mind that God does not just call men to walk in biblical masculinity in their relationships, but also at their jobs, as fathers, as friends, in every aspect of their lives. The same remains true for women encompassing biblical femininity as well.

I don't want to spend a ton of your time explaining what biblical masculinity is not, because I think you can already think of a few ways pretty easily. To give a few quick examples, biblical masculinity is not the abuse of power or authority. It is not roughness or a lack of empathy. It is not a lack of emotion or sensitivity. It is not overpowering the weak or exploiting or taking advantage of the vulnerable. It is not passivity or silence.

When we dig into God's Word, we see that our society in the present day has masculinity all wrong. We, as a society, have made it to where a guy has to worry about being "too masculine" or "too feminine" or "not masculine enough." This is because we can't seem to grasp what God designed men for. A "manly" man is a man who will fight for his marriage and the spiritual wellbeing of his household, but will do it without anger or hostility, and out of complete humility. However, the problem is that women and men both have to realize that God gave men strength, leadership, and different responsibilities than he gave women. A "manly" man doesn't ever use his leadership capabilities, strength, or title for evil, or to induce harm. Like many things, biblical masculinity has been completely distorted because of sin, which is why the script has to be flipped so that it can be redeemed.

Woah, I know. A lot of information all at once.

To be honest, I really feel for men within the church. I know there are times that there seems to be nothing they can do right, or if one messes up, it's on all of them. And for that toxic culture, I am so sorry. I want to acknowledge the fact that men do exist who love the Lord, put him first, and seek to glorify him. There are men who value gentleness and self-control above force and impulse. Men, take that as an encouragement, and women, take that as hope.

Let's go back to the passage previously mentioned: Ephesians 5. I am sure you can recall the verse that commands men to be the head of their wives as Christ is the head of the church. This indeed is talking about leadership and biblical masculinity, but my goodness, it is almost always taken out of context. While people get stuck on this verse, they are reluctant to read down just a few verses where a just as important command is made to men. Verse 25 commands husbands to love their wives as Christ loves the church, and to give themselves up for her, mimicking Jesus' sacrifice for believers.

We so often see these commands as a way for husbands to be selfish and authoritarian over their wives. What we neglect to remember is that the responsibility of a man to be the head of his wife holds just as much weight as his responsibility to love her and willingness to quite literally give his life for her.

Leadership for men is not arrogance, selfishness, or harshness, but rather sacrifice and humility. It is having the humble spirit to admit when you're wrong, confess your sin, and seek wise counsel when you may not have the right answers. It is the willingness to put your wife's life before your own because you have been commanded to lead and love her in a way that mirrors the way Jesus has shown his love to the church.

Just like in the chapter about submission and biblical femininity, I want to specifically point out three things that the Bible says are vital parts in being a man after God's own heart. These are the things that Scripture tells you, men, are non-negotiables when it comes to seeking to live in a way that embraces biblical masculinity. These things come from wise counsel I have sought, messages

I have heard, and ultimately, Scripture. We can pull these qualities from the first man created by God, Adam, in Genesis 2:5-9 and Genesis 2:15-18.

*The first truth: Biblical masculinity looks like pursuit.*

Pursuit, in this context, can be defined and described as taking something that has untapped potential and cultivating that potential into fruition. A man's way of bringing chaos back into order. Pursuing means to leave it better than you found it, and is the opposite of passivity. In Genesis 3:6, we see the turning point of human history: the fall of man. This is where Eve ate the forbidden fruit in the Garden of Eden while Adam was standing right next to her. Yep, Adam was right there, idly watching. This is so crucial because if you look back at this story, you will see that God actually commanded Adam not to eat the fruit, but when he saw his wife disobey God, he did nothing. Adam's actions in this story paint a picture of how detrimental male passivity really is to society. God calls his men to be proactive. Practically, this looks like men investing a concentrated effort towards endeavors in work, school, and relationships. This looks like taking initiative, making the first move, and acting instead of standing by.

*The second truth: Biblical masculinity is the call to provide.*

In Genesis 2:15, we see the purpose of why God placed Adam in the garden: to work, cultivate, and take care of it. It was his job to tend to the plants and wildlife and keep everything alive and well. In today's terms, this means that the people around a biblically masculine man should be well taken care of—flourishing, even. When people are in his presence, they should feel the overflow of God's provision. They should not often feel depleted. Practically, this looks like men going last, and living in the mindset that it is not about them, but rather the people around them. This looks like men working hard to provide for themselves and their family. This looks like stewarding their time, resources, and finances well. And sometimes, this looks like being tired as a sacrifice. Being tired sometimes isn't a bad thing, despite what society may try and instill in us.

*The third truth: Biblical masculinity is the call to protect.*

In the same verse I mentioned before, Genesis 2:15, we also see the word "keep" when God is explaining Adam's job in the garden and on the land. To "keep" means to defend, guard, and protect. We see a bad example of this in Genesis 3:6, when Adam had the ability to protect Eve from the serpent but neglected to. Practically, but also profoundly, this looks like the guy taking the fall so that the girl can go free. I know this is a hard calling and truth, but it's just that: truth.

My last desire for the men reading this is for you to feel discouraged or down on yourself after taking all of this in. I know it may feel like the weight of the world is on your shoulders, but let me remind you that while these things are your responsibilities as men of God, it is not yours to do alone. I have always hated the phrase "God will not give you more than you can handle," because of how far from the truth it actually is. If God did not give us more than we can handle, then there would be no point of Jesus or salvation.

Men, this is not for you to do alone. These responsibilities, while big for you, are what God has entrusted you with to carry alongside him. You can find peace and joy in that. Men cannot perform their roles perfectly, which is why Jesus came to do it and redeem the imperfect.

I will leave you with this:

While sin came from one man, so does redemption.

Rather than leave you with a long list of questions, I simply want to encourage and ask you to reflect on one thing. Thinking back to that story I opened this chapter up with, how would your life be different if you (if you're a man), or if the men around you led with that heart posture instead of the one society tries to tempt men with?

# 9

# Soul Ties

If you grew up in the Bible Belt, or just the Christian church in general, you may have experienced the brunt of toxic purity culture. I know I have touched on this briefly, but because the remainder of this chapter is going to be speaking a lot about sex and purity, I wanted to make sure I define it clearly.

Toxic purity culture is what happens when Christians distort the beautiful, divine idea of purity and make it about shame, exclusivity, and take the Gospel out of God's idea of purity. Many times in Scripture, we read about God's desire for us to remain pure, but it is never about our sex lives alone. In fact, he mentions the importance of purity of spirit, heart, and character way more than he mentions purity in regard to abstaining from sex. Please do not hear me wrong, waiting until marriage is definitely a command we are given as Christians, but in order to redeem what purity culture has become, we have to realize that there is more to it than sex. Purity is a beautiful thing, it is a good thing, but it is not a God thing.

Good things can easily become bad when we make them a God thing and put them on the throne of our hearts where God alone should be. God calls us to be pure in so many areas of our lives, to be set apart, to be holy. This includes our minds, our hearts, how we speak, and our bodies.

The main issue with purity culture and the way it has been distorted is because of the idolatry of purity, therefore glorifying shame. I would argue that the opposite of purity is shame, because God did not create us to know shame. Shame takes our sin and links it directly to who we are, stealing our identity from us. When we allow shame to take over, we lose sight of who our identity is truly in: Jesus.

While yes, Scripture says that God has called us to purity, that does not mean that if we sin sexually, that we are tattered goods and no good for God anymore. Our God sent his Son for the purpose of redeeming our broken spirits. He took on our imperfect records and gave us his perfect one. This is known as the great exchange, and it is the backbone of our faith. Because of this exchange, we can live purely and freely in our identity in God.

Now that we have laid a foundation, we can continue and talk about God's design for sex and marriage. It is so important for us as Christians to not only know what God desires for us in regard to sex and marriage, but to know his heart behind why he created and intended it to be done the way he did. I spoke about this in an earlier chapter, but to refresh your memory, the Bible begins with the union of the first two humans: Adam and Eve. And Scripture ends with the "wedding of the Lamb," Jesus' second coming to earth where he is reunited to his bride: the church. This is a beautiful picture and foreshadowing of how God views marriage. Marriage is an earthly representation of the church's relationship with Jesus. It is a covenant relationship that is self-sacrificing, unconditional, service-focused, marked by love, and a picture of the Gospel. There truly isn't anything else like it. It is exposing and sanctifying all at once.

Marriage is the covenant between a man and woman, to God and each other, to sacrificially love and serve one another until the end of their days on this earth. This looks like daily surrender to Jesus, choosing your spouse despite physical changes or stressful seasons, pursuing the other person like you just started to fall in love, and becoming one in everything you do. In Genesis 2:24, we see God's instruction on this where he describes a man and woman "becoming one flesh." The act of sexual intimacy is symbolic of this, two people becoming one physical being, but also the mingling of their souls. This is where the term "soul ties" becomes relevant.

I know that this phrase can be controversial within the Christian community, but I believe that there truly is something to be said about it. However, I do not believe the idea of it should be used as a shame-provoking scare tactic. The idea of soul ties fully relates to the idea that the physical act of sex does not just increase physical intimacy, but it also invokes emotional and spiritual intimacy between the two people partaking in the act together.

This idea is not solely based on Christianity. In fact, the majority of the people that use the terms would argue that it stems from scientific facts regarding what happens chemically during sexual intercourse. When two people have sex, the bonding chemical of oxytocin and other endorphins are released. Scientists have coined the chemical of oxytocin as the "cuddle hormone" because of the nature of when it is released. Oxytocin is the chemical that is released during childbearing and breastfeeding to bond a child with their mother. It is also the hormone that is released during any time of physical intimacy and during the climax of sex. Doctors and scientists who study this hormone relate it to emotions like empathy, trust, and the building of relationships.

Often, this idea is the basis of why people use soul ties as a tactic to scare people away from sex. I would argue that the last thing we need to do is disregard this idea altogether, but rather we need to redeem it back to how God intended it. While sex is a physical act, it's also a sacred symbol where two souls are being brought together through physical intimacy. It's a demonstration of the privilege it is to be able to completely enjoy another human, your spouse, within a marriage relationship.

Sex is a spiritual thing; a symbol of the covenant of marriage and becoming one with the love of your life. From the beginning of God's Word, he makes it clear that sex is a wonderful gift to us. When we talk about how abstaining from sex before marriage is God's design for us, it is because he has our best in mind always. He doesn't want to deprive you of pleasure.

The redemption of soul ties doesn't look like being scared of sex, or being afraid to have soul ties with someone—it looks like recognizing the beauty that is sex within marriage. It looks like being excited to experience the fullness of Christlike intimacy with someone you have committed your whole being to.

Aside from science, there are many other reasons we know that God views sex as holy, exclusive to marriage, and made for the covenant relationship between a man and a woman. I once heard it put this way: During sex, you are the most Christlike you will ever be. Meaning, God has woman-like characteristics but he also has manlike characteristics. He is nurturing, yet protective. He is just, but also abounding in grace. He is gentle, but fierce. He is convicting, and also encouraging. He seeks to protect, but also provides. During the act of sexual intimacy, man and woman literally become one flesh. A man joined together with a woman in all facets of his being, making these two the most Christlike they will ever be. Not just a man, not just a woman, but one in spirit and in flesh. This is why soul ties exist. This is why God gives us a clear boundary.

One of the main arguments against purity within our society is that it is restricting and it holds you back from experiencing life and the pleasures that come with it. I would argue that purity doesn't promote or enable bondage, but rather freedom.

True freedom is not the absence of restrictions, but the presence of the right ones. This looks like implementing physical, spiritual, and emotional boundaries in romantic relationships to preserve all that you can for your future spouse.

The God that we serve is not anti-sex; in fact, there is an entire book in the Bible specifically about a man's passions regarding his wife intimately. Have you ever considered that he could've made the act of reproduction anything he wanted? He could've chosen to design men and women where all it took was touching fingertips to create new life, but instead he designed us divinely so spouses can enjoy intimacy with one another! It is important to remember that God created sex, and it's a *good* thing. Because God views sex as so divinely created and sacred, he has a specific design for how he meant for it to be; therefore, we should abide by that.

I also want to speak to those of you reading this that have had sexual sin committed against you, or those of you who have engaged in premarital sex. I don't want you to read this and think that this is the end for you. I would rather propose to you that this can be the beginning.

For those of you who have had sexual sin committed against you: I am so sorry. God did not make us for those things, and they are a result of sin and the fall. While God may not have made it happen, he does give us the power of his Spirit to break all bondage, heal all shame, and walk in complete freedom and victory of our pasts. I encourage you to let other people in your community bear those burdens with you. Galatians 6 talks about how we are to carry one another's burdens in the body of Christ. Allow the church to be the church for you.

For those of you who have already crossed the line of premarital sex, your story is not over. Your past sins have already been nailed to the cross and died for. You can repent, and turn away. You have already been forgiven. You are not damaged goods. You are *not* impure.

Hear me again, you are *not* impure.

Jesus makes all things new.

He washes you white as snow.

You can make the decision now to wait on your spouse. Our God is a God of second chances, and he is in the business of providing second, third, and fourth chances.

It is going to be hard, but redemption can be found in him. You are worth no less because of your decisions.

Friends, waiting is hard. And the society we live in glorifies sex, romanticizes it, makes everything about it, and idolizes it to no end. The desires of our flesh can eat us from the inside out if we allow them to. But you can decide whose team you're on and who you are fighting against. In order to die to the desires of the flesh, you have to starve them. Feed your spirit instead. When you feed your spirit through spending time in God's Word, praying, confessing sin, and indulging in Jesus-centered community, you are starving your flesh and feeding the desires that the Lord has for you.

This war is one happening right now within you, you can choose to be on offense or defense.

Sex is a gift. It is sacred, holy, and beautiful within the confines that its Creator gives to us for it.

When we align ourselves with the vision that our Creator God has for us, we walk in true freedom.

Some questions for pondering in regard to sex and intimacy:

1. Is there any practical repentance you need to partake in regarding the way you view sex? Are there boundaries that need to be set with a significant other? (Example: Maybe you need to install blockers on your electronics.)
2. Have I forgiven anyone who has sinned against me or tainted my view of sex?
3. Do I truly believe that Jesus has my best in mind?
4. Do I truly believe that purity and freedom are found in Jesus alone?
5. Am I consistently and fervently waging war in my soul against the enemy to fight to live within God's will for my life?

# 10

# The Best Gift Ever

One of my biggest fears surrounding this book on sex, dating, and relationships, was that no one would listen because of my age and experience (or lack thereof). When I first started praying over this book, I knew the territory that I would be embarking upon was treacherous, touchy, and of immense value. I also had to remind myself that I am merely the vessel, and God is using me to speak his words and wisdom. Since I started writing this, my prayer has been that the words I put on paper would never come solely from me, and that if there ever were words that were mine and not from Jesus, that they would fall on deaf ears and blind eyes.

With that being said, I wanted to make sure I let people who hold more experience in the areas of sex and marriage share wisdom in some way so that I can serve you, as the reader, in the best way possible. I also wanted to make sure that I tried to speak to several different circumstances, because I know that purity culture is toxic, exclusive, and really demeaning in a lot of the Christian world. The last thing I want you to take away from this book and this last chapter specifically is that you are of any less value or worth based on your sexual history. I would be a hypocrite if I communicated in any way, shape, or form that our God is not a God of redemption, and that he can't turn anything into something for his glory. I don't want to pretend like I understand what set of circumstances you're coming from, because I have no idea. And I want you to believe that I would be honored to know you and your story, but because I am not sitting across from you right now, I don't want to dishonor you in any way.

All of this in one blanket statement is: You are valuable despite what you've done or what has been done against you. I prayerfully and carefully try to only speak what I know based off of sole biblical truth. The agenda that people have in regard to toxic purity culture is not remotely the same as my purpose for writing this book, as I am trying to build you up in Christ, and extend the love from him that I have experienced myself.

As mentioned earlier, I wanted to allow others to have the floor in this last chapter, and let you hear directly from Christ followers who have a purity story of their own to share. I wanted to make sure that I had people of all backgrounds and circumstances share, and they all will remain anonymous to honor their confidentiality and privacy.

I reached out to my church family, and people that I know and trust to share not only their experience, but also how God has used their past and present sex life within marriage to edify their view of sex by God's design. I asked them all of the same questions and I am so excited for you to be able to hear directly from them. I have people who are willing to share with you who chose to save themselves for marriage, some that did give into temptation before getting married, and some who have experienced sexual trauma which did not give them the choice, but who have even still seen God's love and grace in spite of the sin committed against them.

I am formatting this question by question, with each letter representing the same person's responses to each question, so that you are able to clearly understand.

My goal for you as I close out this book is to feel encouraged no matter which one of these circumstances you identify with, and to be reminded of God's unconditional love for you.

*Question number one: How long have you and your spouse been married?*

Person A: 21 years.

Person B: Eight months.

Person C: Four years.

Person D: Five years.

*Question number two: How long have you and your spouse been following Jesus?*

Person A: "Seriously, for 20 years, however we grew up in the church."

Person B: "I was saved in 2016 and my spouse was saved in 2014."

Person C: "My husband has been following Christ since he was in middle school (over ten years); I have been following Christ since late high school/early college (around eight years)."

Person D: "I have been following Jesus for twenty-four years and my husband for eleven years."

*Question number three: Did you and your spouse wait to have sex until y'all were married?*

Person A: No.

Person B: Yes.

Person C: Yes.

Person D: Yes.

## Question number four: How did the decision affect your walk with Jesus?

Person A: We both had lots of conviction after falling into sin and allowing our flesh to guide our choices. It took years of battling to forgive myself even though Jesus had forgiven me. Ultimately the void I was seeking to fulfill would be and is only filled by Jesus.

Person B: The Bible says to wait until marriage so I believe as Christians we should honor that.

Person C: It definitely grew me in understanding that our relationship is not about us, but about Jesus. I also didn't feel nearly as much shame in going to Jesus as I had in relationships where I did not follow specific physical boundaries.

Person D: My trust and dependence on the Lord grew volumes. I had dated several guys that claimed a relationship with Jesus and a desire for purity, but they either led to pressures to engage in sexual behaviors or a lack of growth or even existence of faith at all. I had thrown my hands in the air to God and said, "I give up. I should have listened to Paul! A life of singleness, here I come," and was semi-content with it. Then, I met Brett, and he was unlike any man I had ever met, much less dated. He was faithful to the Lord, he trusted his promises, he was obedient in serving and his ministry, and he just loved Jesus more than anyone or anything else. That was different. And I knew pretty soon after meeting him, that God was showing me what a true and genuine man of God looks like and acts like. God was faithful in teaching me more about his goodness, his grace, his love.

*Question number five: How did the decision affect your relationship with each other during dating and engagement?*

Person A: I don't think the effects were fully understood until we understood the gift intimacy truly is and what God designed it to be. It is so much more than we understood. So, the early effects were negative although we did not have a clear knowledge of the big picture until later.

Person B: I believe it made our relationship stronger. We set boundaries to make sure nothing happened. We spent time in the word and in prayer.

Person C: It helped us focus on the relational aspect that comes with dating/engagement, rather than being blinded by the desire or lust involved.

Person D: When we were dating, the boundaries that we put into place taught me to prioritize purity before the Lord because God gave the purest of pure for me, Jesus. Despite the struggles and the desire to be more like other dating couples, the Lord led us through two years of dating and trusting him to lead us and guide us, and he "led us to the altar." I've always found it interesting, that phrase. "Going to the altar" refers to getting married and all the bells and whistles that come with it, and yet we miss the altar part. An altar is a symbol of messy, painful sacrifice all because of unconditional love. That's what marriage, even from the beginning with the wedding vows, points to and is all about: sacrifice. Sacrifices freely given for the other just as Christ gave himself freely for us. Seeing Brett pursue the Lord first and foremost pushed me to pursue my relationship with the Lord more fervently. I began studying God's Word more consistently, praying, seeking encouragement and resolve to maintain our boundaries for the sake of our marriage and even more so the gospel.

## Question number six: Has it made your marriage better, easier, harder?

Person A: The initial battle was harder, but God restored and renewed so much. Not witnessing biblical marriage models as children and young adults made our beginning difficult in ways resulting in us falling into sin.

Person B: It definitely has made our marriage better by honoring God, and honoring each other. It made us appreciate each other a lot more.

Person C: So much better!! It was joy on our wedding night and into our honeymoon because we knew this was something we'd been waiting for and was such a good gift. Plus, the whole "but what if they're bad at sex" thing that same people say is such a lie. Because you love your spouse from a deep-rooted unconditional love, that's not even something that crosses your mind when you wait.

Person D: We trust each other. We didn't pursue sex or intimacy while dating; we pursued the Lord first, which then secondarily led to each other. We didn't make sex and intimacy an idol when dating, which meant we focused more on knowing one another and growing in understanding of the gospel and God's plan for marriage. We discovered that while our individual ministries were good, our gifts from the Lord complemented each other to where our combined ministry as two-to-one, husband and wife, would be a power house, literal walking-image of the gospel. We grew to love each other with the understanding that love is what Jesus did for us. Because we remained steadfast in that purity, we began our marriage free of guilt and shame and haunting memories of past impurities. It's just us in our home, our jobs, our bed.

From the wife's perspective: As a Christian woman, this is a tough question. I love my husband, more than I ever thought I could love another human being, but sex and intimacy have always been difficult for me. Not in a temptation to engage, but rather not to engage. For twenty-five years of my life, I heard nothing but negative things about sex. Sex should not be used as a yell-at-teens card or a go-to-hell scare tactic, but that was my experience as a child and teenager. Sex and intimacy are gifts and blessings from God to man and woman in marriage! But that is not what was taught and explained to me and so many from the pulpit. The church has to do a better job of obediently teaching what Scripture declares about sex and intimacy in marriage. I went from "Don't ever has sex. It's sinful," to "Sex is great! Have it all the time," literally overnight. Even now, I struggle with the lies and foggy teachings of the past, and that sometimes creeps into our marriage. Thanks be to God that he brought me two things: 1) a man faithfully pursuing him that is gracious and patient and loving; and 2) a church with leaders that are faithful in teaching the truths of God's Word about these things.

### Question number seven: What boundaries did you two have set in place, if any?

Person A: We had no boundaries in place.

Person B: We had boundaries. We would leave each other's houses by 10 and also not be alone at each other's houses by ourselves.

Person C: Yes— We had a nightly curfew and also did not do anything beyond kissing. Even making out was off limits. As we moved closer to marriage throughout engagement, we actually had to add more boundaries (not being alone together in our new apartment, not laying down on the couch, etc.)

Person D: *Haha yes!* So many that I can't keep track. We called it Operation: Pillows & Toothbrushes. We would not sit on the same couch alone. If there was no other option, we had to sit at least one seat cushion apart and several pillows stacked in between us, hence the pillow part of the operation. We did not kiss until six months, not even on birthdays or New Years. We were long distance dating the entire time—I had a full-time teaching job, and he was a church intern 2 hours away, which meant we were on the exact opposite of schedules. Our only two options were to meet halfway during the week, and for me to visit occasionally on weekends. Option 1: we would meet halfway in Clinton, SC where there are a total of two restaurants, haha. After the restaurant had closed, we would sit in our cars. We always had to have something in between us in the car, which was 99 percent of the time a deck of Uno cards. In two years of dating, I never once won a game of Uno, but we never once crossed a boundary line either. Option 2: when I would visit him, even though he had plenty of space on the couch or another bedroom at his house with roommates, I was never allowed to spend the night there. I would have to spend the night with the girl interns that I did not know instead, which for me was the ultimate level of discomfort. In fact, we were not allowed in his home together unless someone else was there too. Which is where the toothbrush part came in. I am really bad about remembering to pack all the big items, but I would always forget to pack little things like a toothbrush or deodorant. I was not allowed to keep anything like that at his place. If I forgot, which was every time, we would drive to the local Walmart and purchase the item I'd forgotten. We did a lot of group "dates," because there is power and conviction in community and numbers. We never did any type of Bible study together, which sounds strange, but hear me out. Studying God's Word *together* requires vulnerability, transparency, accountability, and dependency. We knew that all of those things are great to have in a same-gender friend and accountability partner, and in a spouse . . . but not in someone that we were dating. Those are qualities that we looked for each other to have with others, because that showed it could develop in marriage . . . but those things would develop intimacy that we wanted to protect and save for our future spouse. To us, closeness with an opposite-gender person would lead to intimacy and dependability on them, which is a dangerous thing if they are not your husband or wife. See, it's not just about sex. It's about sexual intimacy—sharing yourself with only one person that is your partner in a literal walking-symbol of the Gospel. And we took that so seriously. So we guarded ourselves from sharing that with each other. Also, our relationship and growth in the Lord should not be dependent on another person, particularly someone that we can easily grow to idolize over God. The bottom line is this: it's about sacrifice. It's always going to be about sacrifice. Christ gave himself as a sacrifice for us. Marriage is a constant sacrifice for the sake of the other. So, why should dating not require a level of sacrifice too? I sacrificed some weekends to visit him. I sacrificed my comfortability and pride by staying with people I didn't know. He sacrificed physical touch when, let me tell you, his "love language" is definitely physical touch (love languages are a discussion for another day). We both sacrificed the image of the cute couple to keep our boundaries. But here's the bottom, bottom line—sacrifice for the sake of the Gospel always leads to a much greater reward. Christ's sacrifice made way for my reconciliation back to the Father. Our sacrifices made in marriage point us back to the Gospel for others to see. Our sacrifices to keep our boundaries led to a marriage free of sexual baggage and guilt of our sin. It's just the two of us in our home, our jobs, our bed. Above all, our relationship with each other, though imperfect and still growing, points to a greater, perfected relationship of God's love for his children.

*Question number eight: If you were not a virgin when meeting your spouse or getting married and that was a decision you made, do you wish things were different? If that decision wasn't yours and you were a victim of another person's sin, how has God redeemed that?*

Person A: Of course we would have made a change as neither of us were virgins. I do believe God redeemed it all, but it was painful and so much more difficult than it had to be. But that's sin, and ultimately, we are examples of his goodness and faithfulness. The layers of pain and shame run deep but not deeper than the love of the Father.

Person B: Not applicable.

Person C: When I met my spouse, I was a "virgin" in the technical aspect of not having literal penetration sex. However, I had a prior relationship that was sexually abusive and did pretty much everything BUT the literal definition of sex. It was really really tough getting closer to marriage because I was terrified of doing anything sexual. We had to walk through some really tough stuff during the first few months of marriage, and even beyond, because I had flashbacks every once in a while. But, having a trusting relationship focused on God helped redeem all of those fears so much because my husband would continuously remind me that his love for me is not based in sex. He would stop and pray with me. Overall, the Lord has grown us together so much through this.

Person D: Not applicable.

*Question number nine: What would you tell to middle / high school students who are on the fence about saving themselves for marriage?*

Person A: Please don't give into momentary temptation, I promise it's not worth the lasting effects. I would go as far to say do not date until ready for marriage and don't entertain dating until you have a clear understanding of the other person's values/beliefs.

Person B: It's definitely worth the wait, you don't have to be like everyone else. The world pushes for sin. If you do end up having sex before marriage, you can still be saved and God still loves you. Jesus still died for you.

Person C: Do it!! It's so incredibly worth it. The shame that comes from sexual sin is really really tough to shake. It may feel like it's not a big deal, but it's actually huge. Knowing that you and your spouse have only known one another is such a deep and intimate truth that reflects the way the Lord designed it to be.

Person D: What a loaded question—no way to answer it fully without having a relationship with that student and knowing them specifically.

1. Christ in his pure perfection gave his life in sacrifice for our redemption and reconciliation back to the Father. If we are imitators of Christ, then we should imitate him in this by striving for purity and Christ-likeness and righteousness.
2. Following Jesus requires sacrifice, submission, and humility. Are you willing to sacrifice your desires to follow after Jesus? If the answer is no, the problem is not sex outside of marriage, but the posture of your heart before Almighty God. Salvation leads to sanctification, otherwise salvation most likely has not genuinely taken place.
3. God created marriage as a sacred gift and blessing between that one man and woman. By engaging in sexual intimacy pre-marriage, you are giving away that gift for something that will only temporarily satisfy.
4. Sex was created for marriage. Marriage was created by God to imitate and symbolize our relationship with Christ and his bride, the church. Why would you want to defile this? Is what you desire (sex) more important than God's ordained order and plan? See #2.

Sex outside of marriage is not the ultimate problem—it's humanity's desire to do what it wants when it wants, and consulting God only in emergencies . . . the idol of themselves, the power and authority over themselves and their surroundings supersedes everything else. There are far too many people walking around carrying the title of "Christian," when their lives show no fruit of the Gospel being proclaimed. We cannot teach purity in body if there has not been a purifying of the Spirit first.

I would also walk through various passages of Scripture detailing marriage, what it represents, sex and what it looks like and when it's permissible, etc . . .

## Question number 10: What would you tell them if they had crossed a line in the past and didn't feel worthy or that their story could be redeemed?

Person A: The feeling they are having is something I struggled with for years, but it is finished. Fully surrender and turn away from the sin. He is able to and will redeem you and use you. You are never too late and you are never too far, as long as you lay it ALL at his feet.

Person B: I would be honest and tell them they crossed a line. As humans we fall short everyday but Jesus died for our sins and wants a personal relationship with everyone. God saved Saul who killed Christians and made him Paul.

Person C: The Lord is so so gracious and nothing is too big to be redeemed. Sex in a healthy and loving marriage is so completely different than experiencing it outside of marriage, and if you both love Christ, your spouse will remind you that they love you unconditionally. You may have some tough conversations to work through, but overall, the Lord can use even the most broken stories to create the most beautiful bonds.

Person D: God has redeemed you and bought you with the blood of Christ. Christ in his perfection, gave himself freely . . . FOR YOU! Do you believe this? Do you, in all of your guilt and shame, think you outweigh the perfection and saving power of Christ? Again, sex outside of marriage is not the ultimate problem—it's humanity's desire to live in sin . . . the idol of themselves, the power and authority over themselves and their surroundings supersedes everything else. Someone who has already engaged in this still has this mindset: ME, ME, ME. MY desires, MY wants, and now MY sin. The mindset and belief that ME > God. We have to correct this mindset before confronting the specific sin of sexual immorality. We cannot teach purity in body if there has not been a purifying of the Spirit first. I would also walk through various passages of Scripture detailing marriage, what it represents, sex and what it looks like and when it's permissible, etc.

So, after reading personal testimonies of couples from all walks of life and with Jesus, I hope light was shed on the reconciliation that can be found in the Gospel. Toxic purity culture narrates that sexual sin is the worst of the worst, that if you've ever fallen into temptation that you are damaged goods, and that redemption is for everything else, but not your sexual past. After reading through these responses, I hope you feel seen. I hope you feel empathized with and less alone. In writing this book, I was determined to provide conviction and truth while not allowing it to overshadow the redemption and forgiveness in Jesus. The last thing I wanted was to leave you with hard truths without narrating to you in multiple ways the salvation and love that comes through the Gospel.

No matter your circumstance, past, sin, or anything else, everything you have ever done and will ever do was nailed to the cross with Jesus. He took on your guilt, shame, failures, and shortfalls in order for you to be made pure and redeemed in him alone. Purity in body cannot come before purity in spirit and soul.

As I close out, I want to encourage you in whatever season you are in, and reinforce once again that your worth is in the Gospel alone. Jesus desires for you to have relationships that are edifying, and I am so thankful that we have his Word and Spirit to lay the foundation for that. We serve a God who wants the best for us, and the best for us is life done according to his will and desires.

I am so thankful you stuck along for the ride. This book had some heavy things in it, and my prayer is that you allowed it to stir up things in your heart, and maybe make you a little uncomfortable. The way in which our world views dating and relationships is not the way God wants us to, and I pray that your view was edified through the words that God laid on my heart in this book.

For this last prompt, I want to keep it fairly broad and simple.

*List three lies you believed about Godly dating and relationships before reading this book, and three truths you know now to combat those lies . . .*

One lie:

The truth that combats it:

Second lie:

The truth that combats it:

Third lie:

The truth that combats it:

Made in the USA
Coppell, TX
05 November 2021

65238964R00046